V3/5/80

D0606026

2-81
6-81

An Album of the Fifties

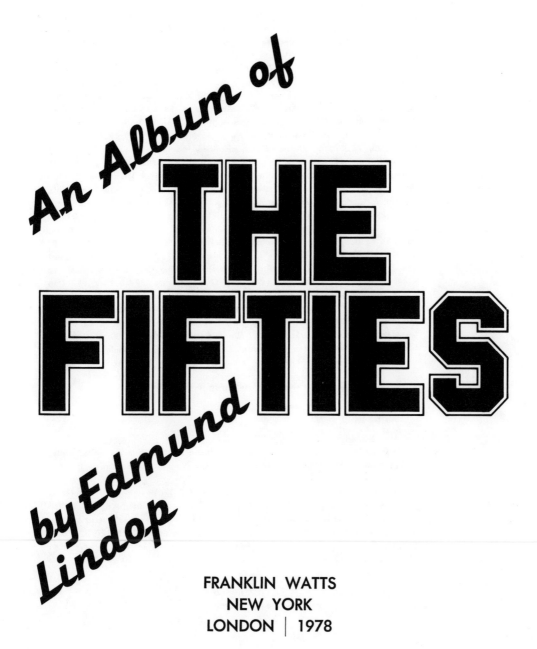

An Album of

THE FIFTIES

by Edmund Lindop

FRANKLIN WATTS
NEW YORK
LONDON | 1978

Cover photographs courtesy of:

Los Angeles Dodgers: front right; Museum of Modern Art Film Stills Archive: front left, back top right, and back bottom left; Friedman-Abeles: back bottom right; National Parks Service, Courtesy of Dwight D. Eisenhower Library: back top left.

Photographs courtesy of:

U.S. Air Force: pp. 14 (top), 32 (top), 39 (top); U.S. Army: pp. 14 (bottom left), 15, 16, 17 (right), 19, 23 (left and right); U.S. Navy: pp. 6 (top left), 14 (bottom right), 40 (top and bottom), 41. United Nations: pp. 6 (top right and bottom), 12 (top and bottom), 18, 27 (bottom right), 28 (left), 46 (left). Dwight D. Eisenhower Library: pp. 22 (left and right), 24, 27 (left and top right), 46 (right); Harry S. Truman Library: U.S. Army, p. 9 (top), Byers, p. 9 (bottom), U.S. Army Signal Corps., p. 17 (left), National Park Services-Abbie Rowe, p. 27 (middle), A.I.D., p. 35 (left and right). Museum of Modern Art Film Stills Archive: pp. 58, 65 (top and bottom), 66 (left and right), 68 (top right and bottom right), 69 (top and bottom), 71 (top and bottom), 75 (left), from the MGM release "Forbidden Planet" © 1956 Loew's Incorporated, 72 (right), Warner Communications Inc., 73. Wisconsin Center for Film and Theater Research: p. 61 (bottom right); United Artists Corp., p. 72 (left); Metropolitan Opera Archives: p. 76 (left and top right); RCA Records: p. 75 (top right); Capitol Records: p. 75 (bottom right); CBS Records: p. 76 (bottom right). Los Angeles Dodgers: p. 86 (bottom); New York Yankees: p. 86 (top left and right); San Francisco Giants: p. 86 (top middle). United Press International: pp. 31, 32 (bottom), 37, 62 (left), 77, 91; Wide World Photos: pp. 25, 45, 52 (left and right), 55 (top), 61 (top, middle, and bottom left), 62 (right), 68 (left), 82 (right), 85, 89 (right and left), 92; The Bettmann Archive, Inc.: pp. 63, 79; Magnum Photos: (Burt Glinn) p. 55 (bottom), (Elliot Erwitt) p. 82 (left); Cushing Collection/H. Armstrong Roberts (Stockwell): p. 44 (left). Northrop University: pp. 39 (bottom), 51 (top right); Texas Highway Department: p. 48 (bottom right and bottom left); Smithsonian Institution National Air and Space Museum: p. 44 (middle and right); Friedman-Abeles: p. 81 (left and right); U.S. Department of State: p. 28 (right); Los Alamos Laboratory: p. 30; General Motors Corp.: pp. 48 (top), 80; St. Lawrence Seaway Authority: p. 51 (top left); Hawaii State Archives/Nancy Bannick: p. 51 (middle); March of Dimes: p. 51 (bottom); American Telephone & Telegraph Co.: p. 59.

Library of Congress Cataloging in Publication Data

Lindop, Edmund.
    An album of the fifties.

    Includes index.
    SUMMARY: Presents the issues and life-styles of the 1950's in the United States including the effects of the Korean and Cold Wars, the civil rights movement, entertainment, and fashion.
    1. United States—Politics and government—1953–1961—Juvenile literature. 2. United States—Social life and customs—1945–1970—Juvenile literature. [1. United States—Politics and government—1945–1953. 2. United States—Politics and government—1953–1961. 3. United States—Social life and customs—1945–1970] I. Title.
E835.L48   973.92   77–14361
ISBN 0-531-01505-X

Contents

Above left: General Douglas Mac-Arthur, standing at the microphone, accepts the surrender of the Japanese government aboard the battleship Missouri. Above right: Secretary of State Edward Stettinius, Jr., signs the United Nations Charter on behalf of the United States. At the left is President Truman. Right: the spectacular headquarters of the United Nations were built in New York City. The building in the center is the thirty-nine-story Secretariat. The General Assembly building is on the left.

Prologue

People in many parts of the world rejoiced on September 2, 1945. That was the day General Douglas MacArthur accepted the formal surrender of Japan aboard the battleship *Missouri* in Tokyo Bay. The Second World War, which had lasted six long years and cost millions of lives, was finally ended. The Grand Alliance—the United States, Great Britain, and the Soviet Union—had brought Germany, Italy, and finally Japan to their knees.

Gone at last were the dreadful fears of bombing raids, invading armies, and somber casualty reports listing loved ones killed, injured, or missing in action. People everywhere looked forward hopefully to a world of peace. A new world organization, the United Nations, had been created in 1945 to make this peace permanent.

Soon after the war, however, disturbing events clouded the rosy prospects for peace. The Russians, who had fought gallantly alongside the Americans and British during the war, launched a dangerous campaign to spread their Communist doctrine. They were determined to gain control over large areas of the world and to force Communism on the peoples who lived there.

(7)

First, the Soviet Union broke its pledge to allow free elections in the countries of Eastern Europe following the war. Instead, Russia turned these nations into "puppet" states, and an Iron Curtain of Communist domination fell over Eastern Europe. The United States could not help these countries behind the Iron Curtain without risking war with Russia.

Greece and Turkey were still free, but in 1947 the Communists tried to extend their control to these two nations. President Harry S. Truman and the U.S. Congress, however, felt that a Communist takeover of Greece and Turkey had to be prevented, and quickly sent in military and economic assistance. This action made it possible for Greece and Turkey to preserve their independence.

The Russians also stubbornly refused to agree with their former allies about the future of defeated Germany. Each of the victorious countries was assigned one zone to govern until a peace treaty could be arranged to reunite Germany. But the Russians never permitted their zone to be merged with the rest of Germany. As a result, Germany remained divided. Eventually it became two countries—West Germany, which was free and democratic, and East Germany, which was Communist-controlled.

An even graver problem was that the city of Berlin lay 110 miles inside Communist East Germany. The city itself was divided into two sections, Communist East Berlin and West Berlin, which became an isolated island of freedom. In 1948 the Communists closed all the highways, railroads, and water routes that ran from West Germany to West Berlin. They believed that when the West Berliners could no longer get food and fuel from West Germany they would be forced to surrender their freedom.

But the United States was determined to prevent West Berlin from falling to the Communists. In June, President Truman ordered the launching of a risky "Berlin Airlift." This airlift flew vast amounts of vital supplies to the people of West Berlin until, many months later, the Communists finally lifted their siege of the city.

Right: as the Cold War intensified, President Truman had to make decisions that were as difficult as those that confronted any American chief executive. *Below:* the Berlin Airlift was one of the most daring peacetime missions in history. Here an American plane is being loaded with food and supplies for the people of the Communist-blockaded city of Berlin.

In Asia, too, fast-moving events heralded trouble for the free world. The Communist forces of Mao Tse-tung emerged victorious in a Chinese civil war. The non-Communist followers of Chiang Kai-shek were driven from the mainland of China and took refuge on the island of Formosa (Taiwan). The Soviet Union now had a powerful ally in Communist China.

Moreover, a divided country emerged in Asia, much like divided Germany in Europe. In the closing weeks of the Second World War, Russian troops occupied the northern part of Korea, down to the 38th parallel. American troops occupied the southern section of the country.

After the war the Russians would not allow Korea to be reunited. North Korea remained a Communist satellite; South Korea became a free nation.

Thus, as the 1940s came to an end, the Grand Alliance was coming apart at the seams. The United States, the strongest champion of the free world, was becoming deeply involved in a dangerous "Cold War" with the Communists. Peaceful relations between Communist and non-Communist countries hung by a fragile thread.

The War in Korea

On June 25, 1950, the Cold War suddenly became hot. Large armies of North Korean Communists, trained and supplied by the Russians, crossed the 38th parallel and invaded South Korea. The aggressors thought that with one swift, mighty blow they could conquer the enemy and reunite the whole Korean peninsula under the Communist banner.

But the Communists faced immediate resistance from both the United States and the United Nations. President Truman quickly ordered American air and naval forces to go to help defend South Korea, and a few days later he sent United States combat troops into battle.

Meanwhile, members of the United Nations Security Council hastily assembled in an emergency meeting. North Korea was charged with starting an unprovoked war against the South. The Security Council then voted that the United Nations take up arms to stop North Korean aggression.

The Soviet Union could have vetoed this resolution, but the Russian delegate was not present when the Security Council voted

to take action against North Korea. Six months earlier the Russian delegate had walked out because the Security Council had refused to admit Communist China to the United Nations. The Soviet Union was still boycotting the Security Council. So, for the first time in history, a world organization voted for its member nations to put down an aggressor who had broken the peace.

Sixteen UN nations sent military forces to South Korea under the command of General Douglas MacArthur, and some forty-one others sent food, clothing, money, and medical aid. The largest number of fighting men, however, came from South Korea and the United States.

(12)

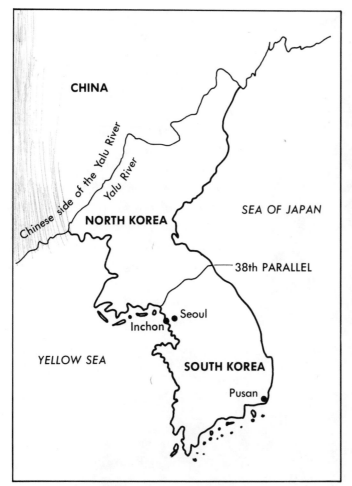

CHINA

Chinese side of the Yalu River

Yalu River

SEA OF JAPAN

NORTH KOREA

38th PARALLEL

Seoul

Inchon

YELLOW SEA

SOUTH KOREA

Pusan

Opposite above: notice that the USSR seat at the Security Council is empty. The Security Council was able to vote UN support for South Korea because the Russian delegate was not present to veto the resolution. Opposite below: President Truman committed all the branches of the U.S. Armed Forces—army, navy, air force, and marines—to the defense of South Korea. This picture shows an army tank column moving to the front.

The North Koreans nearly won the war in its first few weeks. They captured the South Korean capital of Seoul and swiftly pressed forward until they almost reached the port of <u>Pusan</u> at the southern tip of the peninsula.

But by August enough American troops had arrived to reinforce the gallant South Koreans and hold the line at Pusan. Then, the following month, U.S. Marines launched a bold attack around the positions held by the Communists. General MacArthur commanded a surprise amphibious landing at Inchon, a port far to the north of Pusan. This successful invasion above the enemy lines helped UN forces move from the defensive to the offensive.

(13)

Left: the F-86 Sabre jets battled the enemy MIG fighters. American pilots achieved a new record when in one month they shot down sixty-one Russian-built planes, probably destroyed another seven, and damaged fifty-seven others, while losing only four Sabre jets in air-to-air combat. Below right: the U.S.S. Missouri, the same battleship on which the Japanese signed surrender terms in 1945, launches a sixteen-inch salvo against a port held by the North Koreans. Opposite: soldiers in an artillery battalion fire their Long Toms on Communist targets. Below left: this picture shows men in an infantry regiment covering up behind rocks to shield themselves from exploding mortar shells.

Soon the UN armies were sweeping northward, recapturing Seoul and driving the enemy out of South Korea. When the victorious troops reached the 38th parallel, the United Nations directed them to continue into North Korea and liberate it from Communist control. By mid-October the North Korean capital had fallen, and General MacArthur was predicting that his men would soon conquer all of North Korea.

But when the UN forces neared the Yalu, the river that forms the border between North Korea and Communist China, the war suddenly took a new and ominous turn. Hundreds of thousands of Chinese troops poured across the Yalu and drove the UN forces back over the ground they had recently taken. The Chinese charged forward in wave after wave until they had cleared the UN troops out of North Korea.

Left: when the Chinese Communists entered the war, thousands of terror-stricken civilians packed all the roads leading southward. Opposite left: in October 1950, President Truman flew to Wake Island to confer with MacArthur about the Korean War. At that time he awarded the general the Distinguished Service Medal. A few months later Truman dismissed MacArthur as commander of the UN forces in Korea. Opposite right: General Omar N. Bradley, U.S. Army.

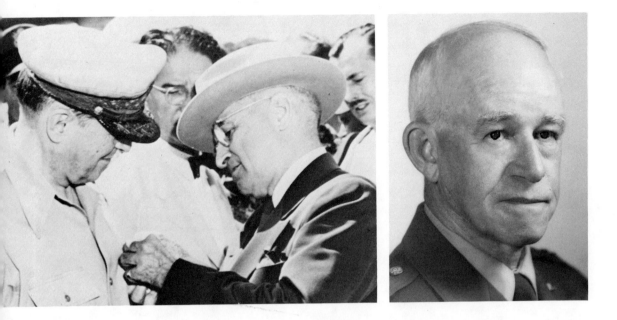

In January 1951, General MacArthur demanded permission to take drastic action against China, including blockading China and bombing of military and industrial targets on the Chinese side of the Yalu River.

President Truman, however, strongly believed that the war should be limited to Korea. He feared that the general's plan to extend military action could bring the United States into an atomic war with China and possibly Russia. The President's position to limit the war was supported by most of his military advisers, including General Omar Bradley, chairman of the Joint Chiefs of Staff.

But MacArthur continued to speak out that there was "no substitute for victory." He maintained that victory would come only by bombing China. When the general wrote to a Republican congressman, strongly stating his position, Truman decided to remove MacArthur from command of the UN forces in Korea.

The country was stunned by the news of the firing. Huge crowds hailed MacArthur as a great hero on his return to America.

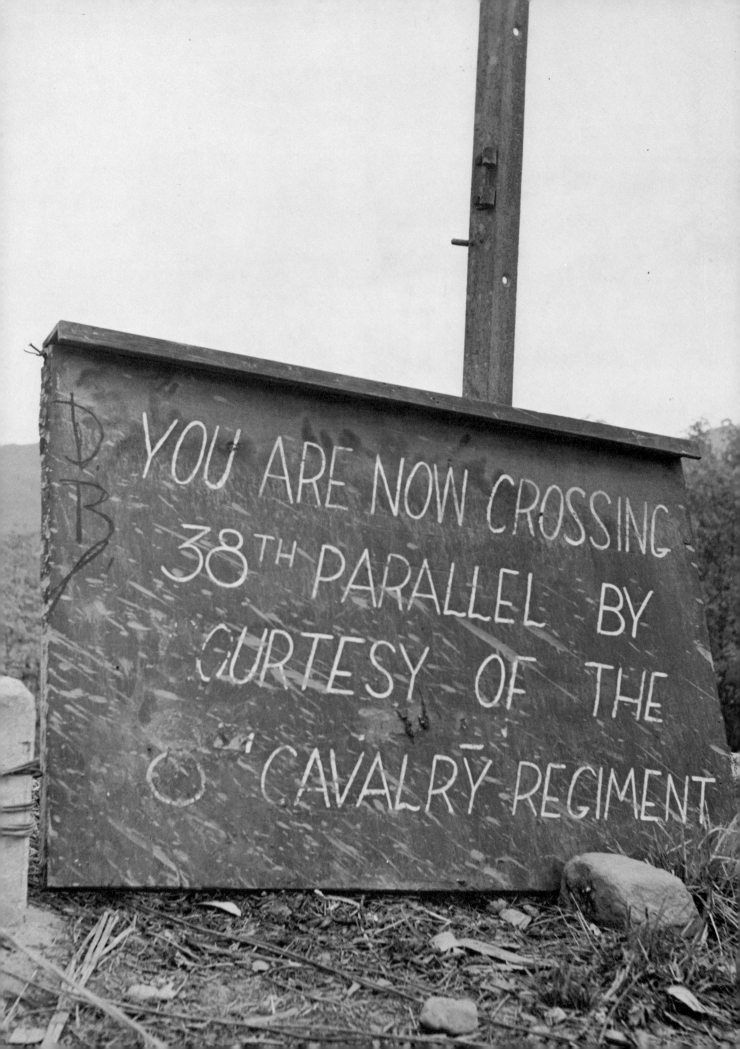

Right: MacArthur made his famous farewell address to a joint session of Congress on April 19, 1951. Opposite: a victory sign left by American forces at the 38th parallel. The peace negotiators drew the new boundary between North and South Korea along a line near the same parallel.

The general defended his opposition to a limited war before Congress and then concluded his address with the dramatic statement that "old soldiers never die; they just fade away." His speech was often interrupted by deafening applause.

While the debate between the President and the general continued to capture public attention, the war in Korea dragged on. In July 1951, negotiators from both sides began talks about ending the war. But peace still did not come to Korea until July 1953 when an armistice was finally signed. The negotiators agreed that the new boundary between North and South Korea would be roughly along the same 38th parallel where the fighting had started three years before.

About two million people were killed or wounded in the Korean War. The United States suffered losses of about 54,000 dead and 103,000 injured.

While neither side was really victorious, the Korean War did prove something important. It demonstrated that through the collective efforts of the United Nations an aggressor could be prevented from conquering another nation by military force.

"I Like Ike"

As the Presidential election of 1952 approached, the Democratic party was in deep trouble. The war in Korea had turned into an agonizing stalemate. Many Americans blamed Truman and the Democrats for this unpopular war. Some insisted that the President had been wrong in recalling MacArthur and in not trying to win the war at any cost. Others claimed we should not have gone into the war at all, and that Truman should not have sent U.S. forces into combat without first getting the approval of Congress.

These criticisms may well have led to a growing belief that the Democrats were "soft on Communism" and that some government agencies employed Communist sympathizers. Further, President Truman and the State Department were accused of selling China "down the river" by not fully supporting Chiang Kai-shek in his futile civil war against the Chinese Communists.

Then, too, there were charges of corruption in the Truman Administration. Assistant Attorney General T. Lamar Caudle had accepted bribes from persons accused of tax fraud. President Truman demanded Caudle's resignation, and Caudle later went to prison for his crime. A Senate investigation revealed that other government officials had taken commissions and costly gifts, such

(20)

as mink coats, for using their influence in Washington to help companies secure government contracts.

In addition to all these criticisms, the Democrats were condemned for their lengthy hold on the White House. Not since 1932 had the country had a Republican President. Twenty years is too long for one political party to control the White House, claimed Republicans, who chanted the slogan, "Had enough?"

One Republican who sought the Presidential nomination in 1952 was Senator Robert A. Taft of Ohio. The son of a former President, Taft was clearly the leading Republican spokesman in Congress. This hard-working, blunt-speaking, highly respected senator had earned the nickname, "Mr. Republican." But Taft, who was greatly admired by the Republican party workers, was too conservative to win much support from Democrats and independents. And his rather drab, uninspiring manner was a serious handicap in attracting enough votes to put the Republicans back in the White House.

Another possible Republican nominee had enormous public appeal, but he was not a professional politician. This was General Dwight D. Eisenhower, whose nickname from childhood was Ike. The son of humble small-town parents, Ike had played high school baseball and football in Abilene, Kansas. Following high school he had won an appointment to the U.S. Military Academy. At West Point Ike demonstrated strong leadership qualities and played halfback on the Army football team.

After college Eisenhower began a distinguished military career that was highlighted by outstanding service in the Second World War. When the war began, Ike was only a major and unknown to the public, but by the time it was over he was Supreme Commander of the Allied Expeditionary Force in Western Europe and the best known, most widely respected hero of the entire war. In fact, Eisenhower was so greatly admired that some prominent politicians tried to convince him to run for President on the Democratic ticket in 1948. But Ike turned down their offer, stating emphatically that he was not a politician.

(21)

Above: Dwight Eisenhower (middle, top row) played on the baseball team at Abilene High School in Kansas. Right: young Eisenhower was a halfback on the Army team at West Point. In one game he played against the great American Indian athlete, Jim Thorpe.

Above: the Supreme Commander in the Second World War talks to his men on the eve of the D-Day landing in France. Above right: Eisenhower was acclaimed as a great hero by huge crowds when he returned home from Europe.

Four years later Eisenhower changed his mind and agreed to enter the race for the Presidency—but as a Republican, not a Democrat. Many of the party regulars at the Republican convention still wanted Senator Taft as their candidate. But the polls all showed strong voter support for the tall, lanky general whose broad smile and soft-spoken manner reflected confidence and sincerity to an adoring public.

The fight for the Republican nomination was hard and bitter, but nonpolitician Eisenhower emerged as the victor. When he delivered his acceptance speech, the convention floor was crowded with signs that proclaimed the message, "I Like Ike."

Eisenhower selected as his Vice-Presidential running mate a youthful senator from California, Richard M. Nixon. A tough fighter on the issue of Communism, Nixon was well liked by the Republican party. But two months after the convention, a newspaper story revealed that Nixon had received more than $18,000 in a secret fund from wealthy California businessmen. The question

Opposite: "Ike" became a favorite nickname of the Fifties, and Republicans publicized it widely at their conventions in 1952 and 1956. Left: Richard Nixon, the Republican candidate for Vice-President, defends himself against charges of possible corruption in the famous "Checkers" speech on television.

was asked whether Nixon had done political "good turns" for the men who paid him this money.

It was embarrassing for the Republicans, who had charged the Democrats with corruption, to discover that their own Vice-Presidential candidate was accused of corruption too. Some party leaders felt that Nixon should be dropped from the ticket. Even General Eisenhower was unsure of what to do about it.

Nixon decided to defend himself in a nationwide television address. On September 23, 1952, he told millions of viewers that the secret fund was used entirely for political expenses and that not a single dollar went into his own bank account. In his dramatic speech Nixon admitted that one admirer had sent him a cocker spaniel dog that his daughter had named Checkers. He said that regardless of what people thought about it, his children loved Checkers, and "We're going to keep [him]."

(25)

The response to Nixon's television address, which came to be called the "Checkers speech," was overwhelming. Thousands of telegrams flooded Republican headquarters, urging that Nixon be kept on the ballot. When Nixon later flew to a meeting with Eisenhower, the general embraced his running mate. With tears in his eyes, Eisenhower exclaimed, "You're my boy!"

Several prominent Democrats competed for the opportunity to run against the Eisenhower-Nixon ticket. The early leader for the Democratic nomination was Senator Estes Kefauver of Tennessee. Wearing a coonskin cap to symbolize that he was the common people's candidate, Kefauver won several important primary campaigns. But many Democratic party leaders, including President Truman, did not want Kefauver as their candidate. Instead, they preferred Governor Adlai Stevenson of Illinois. At first, Stevenson, the grandson of a former Vice-President, was reluctant to run for the Presidency. But a draft-Stevenson movement snowballed at the Democratic convention, and the Illinois governor won the nomination on the third ballot.

Stevenson was a brilliant thinker and an eloquent speaker, but his opponent was almost unbeatable. Eisenhower won the election easily, taking all but nine of the forty-eight states. He polled the largest number of votes ever received by a Presidential candidate. Shortly after the election he kept a campaign promise to go to Korea and try to end the war. His efforts in this area, however, did not meet with immediate success.

Ike proved to be a very popular President. Some critics claimed he did not launch enough bold new plans, but his Administration seemed to suit the mood of the country. Even when he frequently left his desk for golfing games, few people condemned him for mixing pleasure with business.

In 1955 President Eisenhower suffered a severe heart attack, and the following year he was rushed to the hospital for an operation on a blocked intestine. But he bounded back from both illnesses and announced in 1956 that he would seek reelection. The Democrats again nominated Stevenson to run against him.

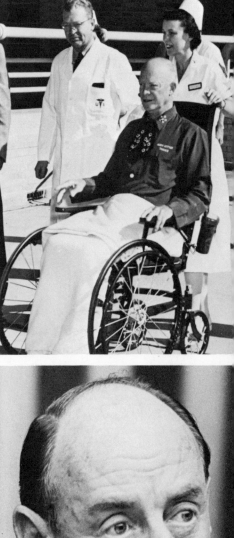

Above: President Eisenhower was one of the most avid White House golfer's in America's history. Middle: in front of the Capitol, Dwight Eisenhower was sworn in as the nation's thirty-fourth President by Chief Justice Fred Vinson. Right above: the nation was stunned when Eisenhower was stricken with a heart attack in 1955. But Ike recovered, and the following year won a second term in the White House. Right below: Adlai Stevenson.

In their rematch Eisenhower defeated Stevenson by an even larger margin than before. Stevenson carried only seven of the forty-eight states. In that same election, however, the Democrats won a majority of seats in both houses of Congress, demonstrating that Eisenhower was far more popular than his Republican party.

Women in both political parties played prominent roles in the Fifties. Mamie Eisenhower was a strong asset to her husband's campaigns and graced the White House as a charming first lady. Sharp-tongued Clare Booth Luce, who was a congresswoman and later ambassador to Italy, became an outspoken leader in the anti-Communist crusade. Eleanor Roosevelt served as a U.S. delegate to the UN General Assembly and continued her lively interest in political and social causes.

Right: Clare Booth Luce. Left: Eleanor Roosevelt remained politically active in the Fifties.

McCarthyism and the Red Scare

In September 1949, reporters were summoned to the White House. As soon as they were assembled, the President's press secretary closed the doors. "Nobody is leaving here until everybody has this statement," he declared. The first reporter to read the press release whistled shrilly and shook his head in disbelief. The statement read: "We have evidence that within recent weeks an atomic explosion occurred in the USSR."

The Soviet Union had the atomic bomb! American scientists knew that the Russians would eventually learn how to make the bomb, but this was at least three years earlier than had been predicted.

When this ominous news reached the public, Americans shuddered with fear and uneasiness. Despite the unfriendly attitude of Russia, the United States had not been in danger of attack as long as it had a monopoly on the A-bomb. But now that the Russians also had it, American security was gravely threatened. When the Korean War began in 1950, there was great concern that the conflict might provide the spark that would set off an atomic war.

(29)

Opposite: in September 1949, the U.S. government learned that the Russians had exploded their first atomic bomb. This photo shows the world's first nuclear explosion, which occurred at a testing range in New Mexico on July 16, 1945. Right: the threat of possible nuclear war forced Americans to consider civil defense measures. These youngsters in Topeka, Kansas, are crouched in a school hallway, practicing survival methods.

Millions of Americans worried about how to protect themselves from atomic bombings. Some began installing bomb shelters in their backyards. Civil defense drills were held in cities and towns throughout the nation. School children practiced huddling in halls or under their desks to shield themselves from the effects of possible bombings.

How had the Russians made the bomb so quickly? This question troubled many Americans, who believed that the Russians were scientifically backward and could not have produced such a weapon by themselves. The Kremlin, many people concluded, must have learned the American "secret" of the bomb. If so, who had leaked this valuable information to the Russians?

Right: this is the kind of nuclear bomb that was detonated over Hiroshima, Japan, in World War II. Very small in size, it was as destructive as 20,000 tons of high explosives. Below: the most sensational spy trial of the decade involved Julius and Ethel Rosenberg, who were charged with plotting the transfer of atomic secrets to the Soviet Union.

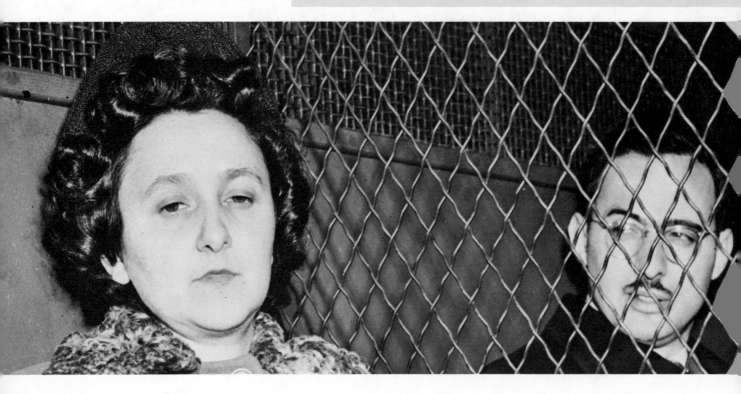

A series of sensational spy cases touched off a wave of hysteria in the United States. In January 1950, Dr. Klaus Fuchs, a British physicist who had worked on the A-bomb in the United States, confessed that he had given atomic secrets to the Soviet Union. Dr. Fuchs was tried for his crime in a British court and convicted. Alger Hiss was accused of passing vital secrets to Communist spies when he had been a high-ranking official in the State Department. Hiss was convicted of perjury in 1950 and sentenced to prison.

Perhaps the most sensational of all the spy cases involved Julius and Ethel Rosenberg. In 1951 they were charged with treason for having plotted to arrange for the transfer of atomic secrets to the Soviet Union during World War II. In sentencing the Rosenbergs to die, the trial judge held them responsible for the casualties in the Korean War. He felt that if the Russians hadn't had the bomb, they would not have supported the Korean Communists in their war effort. To the day of their execution in 1953 the Rosenbergs maintained they were innocent, and some authorities still claim that the couple did not commit treason.

The government began taking drastic steps to protect the United States against Communist subversion. The Justice Department successfully prosecuted eleven top leaders of the American Communist party, who were each given prison terms for conspiring to "teach and advocate" the overthrow of the government. In 1950 Congress passed a tough Internal Security Act, which made it unlawful for Americans to perform any act that might help the Communist cause in the U.S. President Truman authorized a sweeping investigation into the backgrounds and beliefs of all federal employees. By 1952 loyalty checks had been run on over six million employees. A few hundred were dismissed as loyalty risks; another few thousand resigned.

The threat of being called a Communist sympathizer prevented many people from voicing unpopular views or even making controversial statements. The drive to prove a person's "Americanism" was carried to ridiculous lengths. Loyalty oaths were frequently demanded before persons could be hired for jobs that had nothing to do with national security. One state forced boxers and wrestlers to take a non-Communist oath before they could enter the ring. Dearborn, Michigan, staged a beauty pageant in which the participants signed loyalty oaths, and the winner was crowned "Miss Liberty." An attempt was even made in Indianapolis to remove *Robin Hood* from library shelves because of the claim that the book's hero behaved like a Communist, and the name of the Cincinnati baseball team was changed from "Reds" to "Redlegs."

Some Hollywood writers and entertainers were accused of having Communist sympathies. The House Un-American Activities Committee summoned ten film industry figures to testify about any Communist connections they might have had. But the witnesses claimed the Congressional hearings violated their civil rights. When they refused to testify, they were cited for contempt and sentenced to jail. The film industry also punished these and other persons suspected of Communist leanings by "blacklisting" them and refusing to hire them for new assignments.

Richard Nixon first gained national recognition because of his active role in the anti-Communist campaign. During the Alger Hiss hearings, Congressman Nixon constantly fired questions aimed at proving that Hiss had been an agent of the Soviet Union. Nixon also attacked many Democrats in government positions for being "soft on Communism."

But the man who captured the most headlines from the Red Scare that swept the country was Senator Joseph McCarthy of Wisconsin. Before the night of February 9, 1950, McCarthy was a little known, undistinguished senator. But that night, while addressing a Republican rally, McCarthy waved a paper and shouted, "I have here in my hand a list of 205 names known to the Secretary of State as being members of the Communist party and who nevertheless are still working and shaping the policy of the State Department."

McCarthy had dropped a bombshell. He soon became champion of the drive to expose Communists in the government. McCarthy, however, could never produce his list of Communists in the State Department. A Senate subcommittee that looked into his charges concluded that they were a "fraud and a hoax."

But this did not stop McCarthy from making even more wild, irresponsible accusations. He described Secretary of State Dean Acheson as the "Red Dean of the State Department" and Far East expert Owen Lattimore as the "top Russian espionage agent in the U.S." McCarthy charged that General George C. Marshall, chief of the U.S. General Staff in World War II and later Secretary of State, was "an instrument of the Soviet conspiracy."

Two of the men McCarthy accused of being soft on Communism were highly respected former Secretary of State George Marshall and Secretary of State Dean Acheson. Acheson is shown at the left, Marshall at the right.

McCarthy stooped even lower in helping defeat Senator Millard Tydings, who was running for reelection in Maryland. Tydings had dared to speak out against McCarthy, and the vicious Wisconsin senator wanted revenge. So he distributed to Maryland voters a fake photograph that had been made by piecing together a picture of Tydings and a separate picture of the head of the U.S. Communist party.

Although McCarthy never proved any of his outlandish charges, he severely damaged the reputation of many innocent persons. The polls revealed that large numbers of Americans applauded McCarthy for "uncovering" Communists. In truth, he was waging a sinister campaign of character assassination. McCarthy was the master of the "big lie"; mere repetition of his untruths convinced many that he was telling the truth.

The popularity of the Wisconsin senator continued to rise as he smeared one innocent victim after another—until he decided to tackle the U.S. Army. McCarthy accused General Ralph Zwicker of promoting an Army dentist who had refused to answer questions about his political beliefs. Claiming that General Zwicker was "shielding Communist conspirators," McCarthy stormed at the Secretary of the Army, "I am going to kick the brains out of anyone who protects Communists!"

The Army leaders fought back and, furthermore, they claimed that McCarthy had tried to use his influence to gain special privileges for a recently inducted member of his staff. But McCarthy would not back down, and congressional hearings into the controversy began before a national television audience.

Crude, blustering McCarthy finally met his match in a soft-spoken lawyer, Joseph Welch, who was appointed special counsel for the Army. Through careful examination of the witnesses, Welch destroyed McCarthy's case against the Army. Then he successfully pressed the charge that the Wisconsin senator had tried to get special treatment from the Army for his former employee.

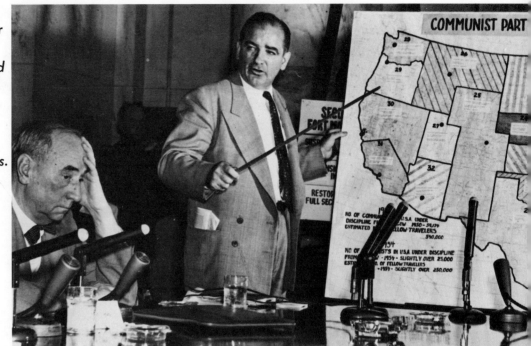

This picture shows Senator McCarthy (standing) and army counsel Joseph Welch during the famous televised hearings.

Enraged and desperate, McCarthy savagely attacked a young lawyer in Welch's firm for once having belonged to a left-wing organization. Welch, his face red with anger, turned to McCarthy and declared: "Until this moment, Senator, I think I never really gauged your cruelty or your recklessness. . . . Have you left no sense of decency?" As Welch walked from the hearing room, spectators burst into applause for the gentle lawyer who had finally vanquished the bully.

In December 1954, the Senate took an unusual step against one of its own members. It voted 67–22 to condemn Senator McCarthy for his abusive actions. From that time on the senator's influence swiftly declined. And with it declined the witch-hunting character assassinations to which the man had given his name—"McCarthyism."

The Cold War Continues

The end of the Korean War did not significantly ease the tension between the United States and the Soviet Union. The Cold War was to continue through the entire decade of the Fifties.

The possibility of a third world war became an even more frightening prospect with the development of awesome new weapons. In 1952 the United States unleashed the hydrogen bomb, a nuclear device hundreds of times more devastating than the atomic bomb. In its first test the H-bomb wiped out an entire small coral island in the Pacific and ripped a hole 175 feet deep in the ocean floor. The following year the Russians had the hydrogen bomb, too. As scientist Albert Einstein observed, the destruction of all life on earth was now "within the range of technical possibilities."

The United States placed strong emphasis on air power. The Strategic Air Command, featuring aircraft that carried the new superbombs, became a major American defensive arm. Guided missiles also became important new weapons in the late Fifties. By 1959 the first U.S. intercontinental ballistic missile was ready for the launching pad.

(38)

Left: in 1952 the U.S. tested its awesome new weapon, the hydrogen bomb. Two minutes after detonation, the clouds rose to forty thousand feet— the height of thirty-two Empire State Buildings. The mushroom pushed upward ten miles and spread over one hundred miles. Below: the SM-62 Snark was the first U.S. intercontinental guided missile.

Opposite: the Navy's new supercarriers held planes large enough to carry nuclear bombs. Below: the launching of the U.S.S. Nautilus. *Right:* the atomic-powered submarines were able to launch missiles either from the ocean surface, as shown here, or while they were submerged.

The U.S. Navy kept pace in the race with the Russians for weapons superiority. Giant supercarriers, which could hold planes large enough to carry nuclear bombs, were constructed. And in 1954 the Navy unveiled its first atomic-powered submarine, the *Nautilus,* which was capable of launching missiles while submerged.

President Eisenhower had a tough-minded Secretary of State, John Foster Dulles, who was determined to stand up to the Communists. Any new aggressive moves by Russia or China, Dulles warned, would be met with "massive retaliation" by the United States. Dulles believed that strategy in the Cold War must include a willingness by the United States to go to the very brink of war if necessary. Critics of Dulles called this policy "brinksmanship," and feared it was dangerous in an era when warfare could lead to atomic annihilation.

In 1954 the United States faced a major decision involving Indochina. The Communists were fighting to free Indochina from the control of France. Both Secretary of State Dulles and Vice-President Nixon wanted the United States to send military forces to help the French hold on to Indochina. But President Eisenhower refused to let the United States become involved in a war there without the support of other countries or Congress.

The French had to pull out of Indochina. Vietnam, which was part of Indochina, was divided into two areas. The northern section was held by the Communists; the southern section was anti-Communist. The United States began pouring vast amounts of economic aid into the new country of South Vietnam, and American "advisers" started training its army. This marked the beginning of American involvement in Vietnam, which finally led to the war there in the 1960s.

President Eisenhower knew the horrors of war from firsthand experience and took some important steps aimed at lessening the threat of a future atomic war. In 1953 he proposed an "atoms-for-peace" plan in which all nations would pool their atomic materials and knowledge for the benefit of humankind. While the Russians did not support this plan, they did agree to the creation of an International Atomic Energy Agency. Unfortunately, this agency did not have the power to prevent the spread of nuclear weapons in the world.

In 1955 President Eisenhower went to a summit meeting at Geneva, Switzerland, where he talked with the leaders of the Soviet Union, Great Britain, and France. Stalin, the long-time dictator of Russia, had died in 1953, and the man who emerged as the new leader of the Soviet Union was Nikita Krushchev. At this meeting Eisenhower made a strong plea for disarmament. He dramatically called for an "open skies" policy by which the four big world powers would allow each other to make aerial inspections of their military sites. Krushchev, however, turned thumbs down to this proposal.

(42)

Throughout the second half of the Fifties, events in various parts of the world threatened to turn the Cold War hot. In 1956 a revolt erupted in Hungary, one of the Soviet satellites in Eastern Europe. At first the Hungarians appeared to succeed in their fight for freedom. But within a few days a huge force of Russian troops and tanks crushed the Hungarian revolt. The United Nations ordered the Soviet forces to withdraw from Hungary, but the Russians paid no attention. The United States, fearful of risking an atomic war with Russia, was helpless to assist Hungary.

In the same year war broke out in the Middle East. Egyptian leader Gamal Abdel Nasser seized the Suez Canal from its British and French owners. Nasser closed the canal to Israel and threatened the same action for other canal users. Later in October 1956, Israel, along with Great Britain and France, invaded Egypt. This sudden attack could have led to a much bigger war, since Russia angrily claimed it would send "volunteers" to help the Egyptians.

Fearful that the Russians might carry out their threat, the United States voted with the Soviet Union at the UN to condemn the military intervention. Under this pressure Britain, France, and Israel agreed to withdraw their forces from Egypt as soon as a hastily organized UN force could occupy the war zone.

The Suez crisis heightened American fears that some oil-rich countries of the Middle East might fall to the Communists. So in 1957 Eisenhower asked Congress for the power to send American forces to stop "overt armed aggression" by Communists in the Middle East if a nation in that area asked for help. Congress agreed, and this new policy came to be called the "Eisenhower Doctrine."

In 1958 the anti-Communist government of Iraq was overthrown and its king slain by a group of army officers who had the support of Russia and Egypt. This action threatened the nearby governments of Lebanon and Jordan, which asked for protection. Putting the Eisenhower Doctrine into effect, thousands of American Marines and paratroopers were hurriedly sent to Lebanon. British paratroopers landed in Jordan.

Again the superpowers drew close to the brink of atomic war. Russia and China threatened to intervene, and the United Nations was hastily convened to consider this new Middle East crisis. A compromise was finally worked out. In return for promises that Lebanon and Jordan would be free from either foreign attack or subversion within their borders, the American and British forces were withdrawn.

Another type of rivalry between Russia and the United States also captured headlines in the late Fifties. On October 4, 1957, the Soviet Union launched the world into the Space Age by sending *Sputnik I* orbiting around the earth. A month later the Soviets scored another dramatic first when *Sputnik II* successfully carried a living dog into outer space. Then, in 1959, came the exciting announcement from Moscow that their *Lunik II* had reached the moon.

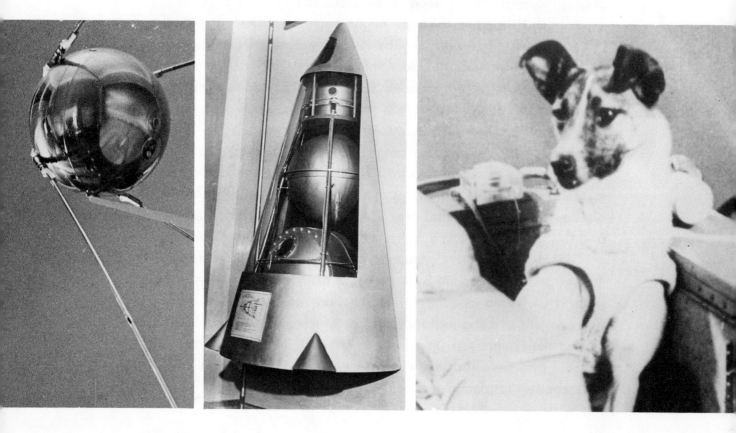

Opposite left: supported by a long, sweeping arch of light metal is Sputnik I. Opposite middle: Sputnik II. Opposite right: the space dog "Laika," prior to launch aboard Sputnik II. Sputnik II went up November 3, 1957. Left: Explorer I puts the U.S. into the space race against Russia in January 1958.

The United States was embarrassed and frustrated to discover that Russia had a long lead in the race to conquer space. After the unveiling of *Sputnik I,* the American government gave a high priority to its own rocket development. Finally, in January 1958, the Army's Jupiter rocket, *Explorer I,* put the United States into the space race. Later the nation heard President Eisenhower's 1958 Christmas message relayed by satellite from outer space. Still, these were modest achievements compared to those of the Soviet Union.

(45)

Left: the head of the Russian government, Nikita Krushchev, visited the U.S. in 1959. Far left: shortly after Fidel Castro gained control of Cuba, he began to denounce the U.S.

Krushchev was still boasting about Russian exploits in space when he visited the United States in 1959. But in return the U.S. had some surprises for him. Krushchev could scarcely believe the large number of Americans who owned automobiles, television sets, and electric dishwashers. And he was astounded to discover that most of these prosperous-appearing people were ordinary folk working in factories, offices, and stores.

Near the end of the Fifties, the United States was disturbed by still another international problem, this time within the Western Hemisphere. On January 1, 1959, Fidel Castro and his followers triumphed in their five-year war to gain control of Cuba. Soon Castro began denouncing the United States, seizing American-owned property in Cuba, and seeking the financial and military support of Russia.

Before long Castro had turned Cuba into a Communist island, just ninety miles from the United States. As the Fifties gave way to the Sixties, Communist Cuba, backed by the Soviet Union, became a trouble spot for the United States.

(46)

Prosperity at Home

Never before had the United States enjoyed such great economic growth as it did in the Fifties. Except for brief recessions at the end of the Korean War and in 1957–58, the country experienced unrivaled prosperity.

The Gross National Product, which is the total of all the nation's goods and services, climbed from $318,000,000,000 in 1950 to an astounding $503,000,000,000 in 1960. The number of jobholders rose from about 53 million in 1950 to over 70 million by 1960. Moreover, the average family income climbed steadily during the decade.

Stock market prices reached a record high. Basic industries, such as steel and oil, operated at near capacity. There also were some major new industries, such as computers and electronics (which added words like "hi-fi" and "transistor" to our vocabulary).

But technological developments were changing the character of many industries. While automation and computers could replace the drudgery of many chores, they threw out of work the men and women who had previously performed these chores.

(47)

Above: an aerial view of a shopping center built in the 1950s near Houston, Texas. Right: an aerial view of a freeway cloverleaf built in Texas in the 1950s. Top: this elegant car is the Cadillac Eldorado Brougham. It sold for over $13,000, and sported a dashboard equipped with a vanity case, lipstick, tissue box, and four gold-finished drinking cups.

During the Fifties the movement of people from the cities to suburbs greatly accelerated. In the first five years of the decade, suburbs grew seven times as fast as the central cities. Many reasons were given for deserting the cities for suburbs—cleaner air, less noise and traffic, more green lawns and trees, better schools, less crime. To shop for the family the suburban housekeeper no longer needed to fight downtown traffic, since newly built nearby shopping areas housed a variety of stores and offices that provided all the goods and services needed. Meanwhile, many inner cities waged massive campaigns to tear down old shabby buildings and replace them with modern structures. Up went new skyscrapers, factories, apartment houses, government-funded low-cost housing, and new schools.

The Federal Highway Act of 1956 provided billions of dollars to construct a modern interstate highway system. These new highways were sorely needed because the production and use of cars increased tremendously in the Fifties. Not only were more people driving to work, but millions were also taking to the road for vacation trips. In the summer of 1957, for example, over half of the American people loaded their cars with suitcases and took off for motoring vacations. The production of new cars in the Fifties broke all existing records.

Sports cars appealed to those people who regarded driving as pleasure. Chevrolet's Corvette was one of the most popular sports cars. Other cars people especially liked were the Thunderbird, Jaguar, Triumph, MG, Sprite, and Austin-Healey.

The Fifties was the first decade when European compact cars flooded the American market. Mileage economy, low cost, and the ease of parking all were reasons for the popularity of small cars. These foreign cars caught on so fast with the buyers that soon American companies began producing compacts, too.

(49)

Just as more people took to the road in the Fifties, so did more people take to the air routes. During the decade about 90 million Americans traveled by air to many parts of the world and spent $17,000,000,000 on their trips. Near the end of the decade, jet transport planes were introduced, and they revolutionized the airline industry. Travel time was cut about in half; jets streaked across the continent in four and one-half hours and over the Atlantic in seven hours.

One of the greatest engineering feats of the Fifties was the construction of the St. Lawrence Seaway, stretching from Lake Superior to the Atlantic. It opened in 1959 and linked the navigable waters of the St. Lawrence River and the Great Lakes by three series of locks. For the first time the St. Lawrence Seaway opened the industrial and agricultural areas of the Middle West to large ocean vessels. By way of the seaway and the great circle route, Detroit, Michigan, became four hundred miles closer to Amsterdam, Holland, than New York is.

There also were impressive achievements in medicine in the 1950s. In 1954 Dr. Jonas Salk introduced a new polio vaccine in a nationwide test among nearly two million children. The Salk vaccine proved so effective that the polio rate dropped dramatically. Important advances were also made in other medical fields, such as kidney transplants, heart surgery, cancer research, and the use of laser beams in surgery.

Another major accomplishment of the Fifties was the addition in 1959 of two new states to the United States—Alaska and Hawaii. For the first time in its history two territories that did not border the continental United States became full-fledged states in the Union. Just as many other industries boomed in the Fifties, the flagmakers were suddenly flooded with orders when the United States changed from forty-eight to fifty states.

(50)

Above right: the introduction of jet passenger planes revolutionized the airlines industry. This is a picture of the first Boeing 707. Above left: this picture shows the construction of some of the locks for the St. Lawrence Seaway. A great engineering achievement, the Seaway opened the Middle West to ocean vessels. Left: a major medical achievement of the Fifties was the successful Salk vaccine for polio. Here Dr. Jonas Salk is administering his vaccine to a youngster. Middle: the Hawaiian people celebrated when their homeland became the fiftieth state.

Above: Mrs. Rosa Parks, the black seamstress whose refusal to move to the back of the bus touched off the bus boycott in Montgomery, Alabama, is fingerprinted by the police.
Right: the Reverend Martin Luther King, Jr., a leader in the Montgomery bus boycott, walks away from the courthouse after being arraigned along with eighty-eight other blacks.

The Civil Rights Movement Advances

A middle-aged black seamstress was riding the bus home from her job one day. She was tired at the end of a day of hard work, and when a white man boarded the bus she refused to stand up and give him her seat. Soon afterward the woman, named Rosa Parks, was arrested for breaking a Jim Crow law that said that when a bus was crowded the black riders had to give their seats to white passengers.

This incident occurred on December 1, 1955, in Montgomery, Alabama, and in that same city at the same time was a young black minister, Martin Luther King, Jr. To protest the woman's arrest, King called together a group of black leaders in Montgomery. They decided to boycott the city buses and wage an all-out campaign to desegregate public transportation.

Soon the blacks quit riding the buses. Some walked to and from work, often as far as ten miles. Others formed car pools that involved hundreds of automobiles. The boycott proved very successful. Before long the bus lines and many businesses in Montgomery were reporting heavy losses.

(53)

White segregationists tried many tactics to break the boycott. Employers threatened to fire black workers who would not ride the buses. Sometimes white gangs beat up blacks who were standing on curbs waiting for car rides. The leaders of the boycott were arrested on trumped-up charges, and King's own home was bombed in an ugly attempt to frighten him.

In spite of all the abuses and dangers that confronted the blacks, King insisted that his people react without violence. But they did not give up the boycott until nearly a year later, when the Supreme Court declared bus segregation unconstitutional.

In 1954 the Supreme Court had made another significant decision affecting civil rights. That was when the Court finally struck down the law on which the South had maintained its segregated school system. In *Brown* vs. *Board of Education of Topeka,* Chief Justice Earl Warren delivered the unanimous opinion of the Court. "We conclude that in the field of public education," Warren declared, "the doctrine of 'separate but equal' [schools] has no place. Separate educational facilities are inherently unequal."

Some border states acted almost immediately to integrate their schools. Most Southern states, however, used various methods to try to block the Court ruling. Little Rock, Arkansas, was a major center of resistance. In 1957 Arkansas Governor Orval Faubus directed his state's National Guard to prevent nine black students from enrolling at Little Rock's Central High School.

President Eisenhower refused to let Governor Faubus defy the Supreme Court ruling. He ordered the Arkansas Guard into federal service, which took it away from the control of the governor. In addition, the President sent a regular U.S. Army unit to Little Rock. With fixed bayonets, the troops stood guard over the blacks who attended the school. At first the black students were jeered, spat upon, and jostled in the halls. But they bravely kept going, and by the end of the school year the people of Little Rock were peacefully accepting integration.

Above: decisions by the Supreme Court advanced the cause of civil rights during the Fifties. Seated, left to right: William O. Douglas, Hugo L. Black, Chief Justice Earl Warren, Felix Frankfurter, and Tom C. Clark. Standing: Charles E. Whittaker, John M. Harlan, William J. Brennan, Jr., and Potter Stewart. Right: federal troops escorted black students to Central High School in Little Rock.

In 1957 Congress passed the first civil rights act in eighty-two years. It provided federal protection to blacks who wanted to vote in the South. The act also created a Commission on Civil Rights to investigate areas where blacks were being prevented from voting.

As the decade of the Fifties ended, there was still discrimination against blacks in both the South and North. But the movement to provide equal rights to all Americans had taken some big steps forward.

Television Comes of Age

In 1948 there were less than 17,000 television sets in the United States. By the end of the 1950s, Americans owned about 50 million. Nearly ninety percent of all American families had televisions, and many had more than one set. Within a single decade television was to become the most important communications industry.

The television revolution caused mixed reactions. Some critics called TV the "idiot box" or the "boob tube," and claimed that most of the shows had little value. Educators feared that the home screen kept children from reading and doing their homework. They deplored the violence and sex that often were depicted in crime shows, Westerns, and adult plays adapted for television. It was estimated that more people were murdered on TV in the single year of 1954 than the U.S. lost in the entire Korean War.

Television changed the life-style of millions of people. TV viewers tended to stay up later at night and leave home less frequently. But this did not necessarily mean that families became any closer. With the invention of the frozen "TV dinner" in 1954, family members did not even have to talk to each other during supper.

(57)

Television commercials became a huge business, accounting for about $1,500,000,000 in advertising money to over six hundred stations. But not every viewer watched the TV ads closely. In 1954 the water company of a large city became puzzled as to why water consumption rose so significantly during certain three-minute periods. A survey revealed the answer—people in that city were all flushing their toilets during the TV commercials.

In spite of the low quality of some of its shows, television brought many important events into the living rooms of ordinary citizens. The first coast-to-coast telecast in September 1951, brought live coverage of President Truman addressing the opening session of the Japanese Peace Treaty Conference in San Francisco. Thanks to television, Americans had ringside seats at political conventions and both inaugurations of President Eisenhower. When *Hamlet* was shown on TV screens in 1953, more people watched it at home than had seen it on the stage in the 350 years since it was written.

Opposite: after television invaded most American homes in the Fifties, many theaters, like the one shown here, had to be converted to other uses. Right: the first TV transmission over transcontinental radio-relay featured President Truman as he opened the Japanese Peace Treaty Conference in San Francisco in 1951.

Television news coverage became a living newspaper; people could actually see and hear the daily headlines. Probably the best known commentator of the Fifties was Edward R. Murrow, whose CBS half-hour news show ranged over the globe from Lebanon to Cuba. Other popular news broadcasters included the NBC pair, Chet Huntley and David Brinkley, and the ABC team headed by John Daly.

The versatile Daly also hosted one of TV's most durable quiz shows, "What's My Line," which made its debut in 1950 and continued uninterrupted for over seventeen years. Other quiz shows with large audiences included "I've Got a Secret," "The Price is Right," and for music fans, "Name That Tune." The first of the big money quiz shows was "The $64,000 Question," in which contestants answered questions in isolation booths. Psychologist Joyce Brothers was the most famous contestant on this show. She won in the category of boxing.

The richest quiz show, however, created one of the biggest scandals of the decade. On "Twenty-One," if a player answered correctly and chose to keep going, the questions grew harder and the prize money grew larger. Charles Van Doren, a handsome young college instructor, dazzled the public by answering question after question until he amassed a record payoff of $129,000. Van Doren became an instant celebrity known to millions of viewers as a walking encyclopedia. In 1958, however, the bubble burst when a congressional investigation revealed that the show was a fraud. Van Doren and other contestants, it was discovered, had been given the questions in advance.

But in the early Fifties the two biggest names in television were Ed Sullivan and Milton Berle. Sullivan hosted a CBS variety show that featured all types of entertainers, from Broadway actors and opera singers to acrobats and performing dogs. Berle, the slapstick comedian, was nicknamed "Mr. Television," and for five years his was the top-rated show on TV.

Below: a popular team of television news broadcasters were Chet Huntley (left) and David Brinkley. Right: the biggest television scandal in the Fifties involved Charles Van Doren. A congressional investigation revealed that Van Doren and other contestants on a big-money quiz show had been given the questions in advance. Bottom left: to millions of TV fans comedian Milton Berle was known as "Mr. Television." Bottom right: Ed Sullivan played host to a wide variety of distinguished guests.

Perhaps the most popular show for most of the decade was "I Love Lucy," which featured the husband-and-wife comedy team of Lucille Ball and Desi Arnaz. Zany Lucy, always with the best intentions, managed to constantly get involved in hilarious predicaments that delighted her fifty million weekly television fans.

There was a variety of shows in the Fifties to suit the varied tastes of television viewers. For Western fans there was "Gunsmoke," "Wagon Train," "Have Gun, Will Travel," "Wyatt Earp," and "Cheyenne." Jack Webb's "Dragnet" was probably the most watched crime-busting show. For fans who liked the spectacular, the top attraction of the decade was the first network presentation of a Broadway production, *Peter Pan*. An estimated sixty-five million people watched Peter, played by Mary Martin, fly through the air suspended on wires. For teenagers, Dick Clark's "American Bandstand" kept them up-to-date on the latest dances.

Opposite right: Everyone seemed to love "I Love Lucy," which starred Lucille Ball (under the table), her husband Desi Arnaz (right), and their sidekicks William Frawley and Vivian Vance. Opposite left: Dick Clark, emcee of "American Bandstand," became known as America's oldest teenager. Left: Lassie captured the hearts of nearly all who watched her perform.

The children had their special shows, too. Among them were "Kukla, Fran and Ollie," which featured the clever antics of puppets, "Captain Kangaroo," "Howdy Doody," and "Lassie." The "Disneyland" series began in 1954, and it alternated adventure tales such as "Davy Crockett" with shows that portrayed the famous Disney cartoon characters.

Perhaps the best live dramas ever produced for television were seen on home screens in the Fifties. In that decade motion picture studios refused to provide television with their old films, so the broadcasting studios had to create their own stories, or adapt plays and novels for TV. Some of the best known of these were the "Hallmark Hall of Fame," "Playhouse 90," "Kraft Television Theatre," "Philco Playhouse," and the "U.S. Steel Hour."

The television industry grew from infancy to gigantic proportions during the Fifties. In many ways this decade was the golden age of TV.

MOVIES

The television boom in the Fifties dealt a serious blow to the movies. So many people stayed home and watched shows on their own screens that thousands of movie theaters had to close their doors. Motion picture attendance dropped from sixty million in 1950 to forty-two million in 1959.

But Hollywood fought back with a series of technical innovations. The first was Cinerama, which used three projectors on a huge screen and made viewers feel they were participating in all the exciting action they saw. Next came three-dimensional films, which blended the images produced by two studio cameras and two projectors. Viewers watched 3-D films with special polarized glasses, and they were intrigued by the illusion of depth portrayed on the screen. But 3-D films generally lacked artistic quality and proved to be a passing fad.

The movies of the Fifties were different in many ways from the movies of earlier years. In the Forties Hollywood provided many glamorous films that were frothy, lighthearted tales of make-believe. In the Fifties films focused more on creating realism.

(64)

Right: as people watched this Cinerama scene, they felt as if they were riding the roller coaster too. Below: in order to experience the illusion of depth in a 3-D film, the audience had to wear special polarized glasses.

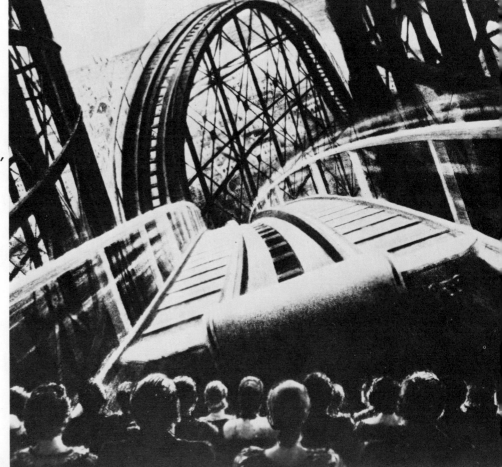

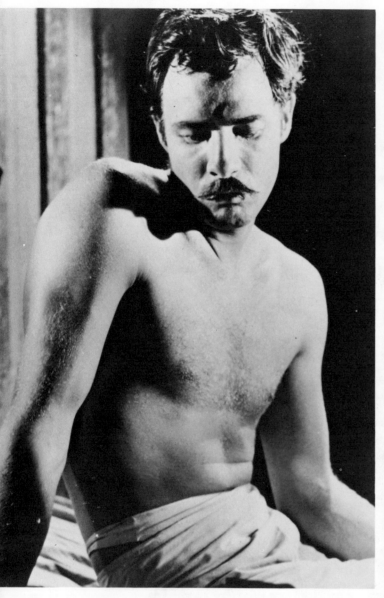

Above: Marlon Brando played in many major productions. Here he is shown as a Mexican leader in Viva Zapata. Right: James Dean was one of the teenagers' favorite actors. Here he is seen in East of Eden.

Marty (1955) was a good example of the new realistic films produced by Hollywood. The central character, enacted superbly by Ernest Borgnine, was a shy, lonely person who faced the typical, everyday problems that confront many of us. Another strongly realistic film was *A Streetcar Named Desire* (1951) in which Marlon Brando portrayed a brutish man who both fascinated and repelled audiences. Brando's role vividly impressed teenagers because it reflected their own frustration at a society that they could not understand or appreciate.

James Dean was another young actor with whom many adolescents identified. He introduced to films the concept of the teenage rebel, which in real life was expressed by street gangs who raced hotrod cars and motorcycles. In his most famous films, *Rebel Without a Cause* (1955) and *East of Eden* (1955), Dean played the sensitive, restless youth struggling against a world of conformity.

Among the actresses, no one matched Marilyn Monroe as a box office attraction. She was the sex symbol of the decade. Shapely Marilyn was usually cast in the role of a naive blonde constantly being pursued by adoring males. Her most skilled performance was in *Bus Stop* (1956), and she also starred in *Gentlemen Prefer Blondes* (1953), *The Seven Year Itch* (1955), and *Some Like It Hot* (1959). Other glamorous leading ladies of the decade included regal Grace Kelly and beautiful Elizabeth Taylor.

Two of the best musicals of the Fifties were *An American in Paris* (1951), with Gene Kelly, and *The King and I* (1956), starring Yul Brynner and Deborah Kerr. One of the finest Westerns ever made was *High Noon* (1952), which swept the Academy Awards.

When Hollywood technicians developed Cinemascope with its wide, angle-curving screen, it was possible to show very large scenes. The first movie in Cinemascope was *The Robe* (1953), a lavishly produced biblical story about what happened to Christ's robe. This started the trend toward making spectacular films, known

Right: Sidney Poitier was one of the first important black film stars. This picture shows Poitier and John Cassavetes in Edge of the City. Opposite left: Marilyn Monroe rehearsing for a scene in The Seven Year Itch. Opposite above right: later to become a real princess, Grace Kelly looked regal as shown here in The Swan. Opposite below right: in the Fifties Elizabeth Taylor was already a leading lady in films. Here she is shown in The Last Time I Saw Paris. Above: one of Hollywood's greatest musicals of the Fifties was The King and I, starring Deborah Kerr and Yul Brynner.

as "blockbusters," which featured vast panoramic scenes crowded with hundreds of actors. These spectacular movies were expensive to produce. Cecil B. DeMille's *The Ten Commandments* (1956) cost $13,000,000. *Ben Hur* (1959), with its cast of 25,000, was even more expensive, but it was a box office success and won nine Academy Awards.

Science fiction films were an important part of the Fifties film scene. *Destination: Moon* (1950) told about man's first moon landing nineteen years before this mission was accomplished. The public was intrigued with the idea of space travel, and this film helped audiences visualize what would be involved in an actual space flight.

People were also fascinated and frightened by the spectre of atomic bombings. *Five* (1951) described what might happen to those left alive after an atomic holocaust. In *The Day the Earth Stood Still* (1951) a space man and a robot landed in Washington, D.C., in a flying saucer. Unless the space man's command to stop using atomic power was followed, the robot would obliterate the earth.

Invasion of the Body Snatchers (1956) was a bloodcurdling science fiction film. It portrayed large armies of cruel, emotionless, podlike creatures arriving from space. Each pod could assume the shape, then take over the mind of some person on earth.

A possible effect of atomic fallout was the theme of *The Incredible Shrinking Man* (1957). In this film a man is engulfed by radioactive dust. It causes him to shrink smaller and smaller. For a while the tiny person lives in a dollhouse. But he continues to grow even smaller. In the end he shrinks out of sight and joins the mass of microscopic particles floating in space.

Among the other popular science fiction films were *This Island Earth* (1955), *Forbidden Planet* (1956), and *On the Beach* (1959). Many consider that during the Fifties enthusiasm for science fiction movies reached its peak. Interest in this type of film waned in the Sixties and was not revived again until the late Seventies.

*Above: Destina-
tion Moon (1950)
was America's
earliest major
movie about
lunar exploration.
Right: Kevin
McCarthy tries
to stop* The Inva-
sion of the Body
Snatchers *before
it's too late.*

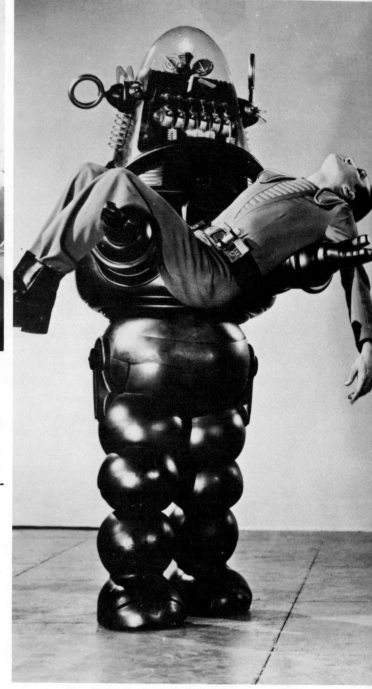

Opposite: one possible conse-
quence of the misuse of atomic
power is portrayed in Them.
Right: Forbidden Planet starred
one of America's most beloved
robots, Robby. Above: perhaps
the most frightening of the post-
bomb movies was the poignant
tale of On the Beach starring
Gregory Peck, Ava Gardner,
and Fred Astaire.

THEATER

Broadway provided some outstanding productions by established playwrights in the 1950s. These included Arthur Miller's *The Crucible* (1952), Eugene O'Neill's *Long Day's Journey Into Night* (1956), and Tennessee Williams's *The Rose Tattoo* (1950), *Cat On a Hot Tin Roof* (1954), and *Sweet Bird of Youth* (1958). A promising new playwright was William Inge. Theatergoers flocked to see his trio of plays, *Picnic* (1952), *Bus Stop* (1954), and *The Dark at the Top of the Stairs* (1957).

Other great plays of the decade include *Diary of Anne Frank* (1955), which told about a teenage Jewish victim of Nazi persecution, the stage adaptation of Thomas Wolfe's powerful novel, *Look Homeward, Angel* (1957), and the story of Helen Keller as depicted in *The Miracle Worker* (1959).

Probably the best musical show of the decade was *My Fair Lady* (1956), which broke all the box office records. Other popular musicals included *Guys and Dolls* (1950), *The Music Man* (1957), *West Side Story* (1957), and *Sound of Music* (1959).

MUSIC

The type of music that captivated teenagers was rock-and-roll, which blended country-Western ballads with black rhythm-and-blues. The most popular idol of young girls was Elvis Presley, who sang rock-and-roll tunes while strumming an electric guitar and swinging his hips. By 1960 fans had bought about $120 million worth of Presley records, sheet music, and products endorsed by their hero. Other popular recording artists of the Fifties included Eddie Fisher, Harry Belafonte, Fabian, Debbie Reynolds, Peggy Lee, and Rosemary Clooney. Many of the records sold were the new "45" type, which were much smaller than the old standard records.

Left: hip-swinging, guitar-strumming Elvis Presley was the teenagers' heartthrob in the Fifties. Top right: calypso singer Harry Belafonte was one of the decade's most popular recording artists. Bottom right: Peggy Lee was a favorite female singer.

For classical music lovers there was Leonard Bernstein, who gained fame as a composer, pianist, and conductor of the New York Philharmonic Orchestra. A young pianist, Van Cliburn, achieved international acclaim when he won first place in Moscow's International Tchaikovsky Piano Competition. And the Metropolitan Opera House made history by featuring its first black singer in a leading role, the wonderful coloratura, Marian Anderson, and by introducing the flamboyant soprano, Maria Callas, to American audiences.

Right: Leonard Bernstein, composer, pianist, and conductor. Top right: Marian Anderson, here shown as Ulrica in Un Ballo in Maschera. *Above: Maria Callas, in* La Tosca. *Opposite: Pablo Picasso.*

ART

Art interest reached a new pinnacle of popularity in the Fifties. In 1956 over one million visitors went to Rotterdam, Netherlands, to view a large collection of paintings by the great Dutch artist, Rembrandt, in celebration of his 350th birthday.

Pablo Picasso, Diego Rivera, and Andrew Wyeth were three well-known artists whose works were exhibited in many countries. Amateur painters who attracted interest included President Eisenhower and Sir Winston Churchill.

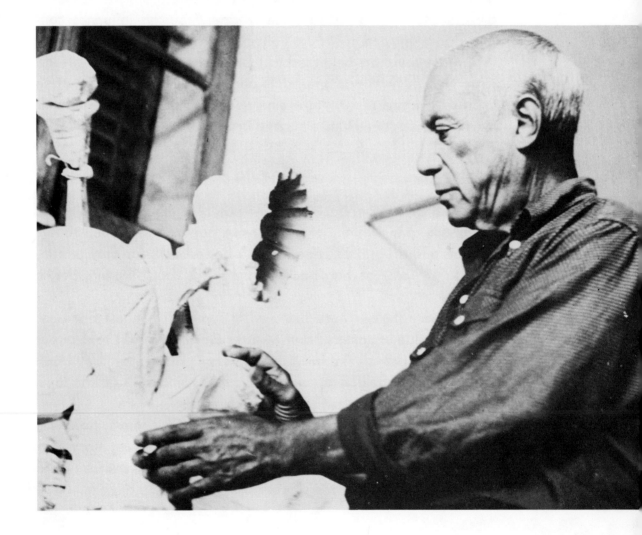

The most important development in art in the Fifties was perhaps the increasing use and acceptance of abstractionism. Many people still viewed an abstract painting or form of sculpture with bewilderment and turned away in disgust. But others developed an appreciation for abstract art and captured the spirit of the work without concerning themselves about its literal meaning.

Jackson Pollock was the leader of the American abstractionist school. This talented nonconformist dripped paint on the canvas with a stick or sometimes splattered it directly from a can. Those who were unimpressed by Pollock's work described it as nonsense and labeled the artist, "Jack the Dripper." But his influence continued to grow, and in 1960 a Pollock canvas sold for $100,000.

Many sculptors belonged to the abstractionist movement and experimented with new materials and shapes. Unusual and often impressive forms of sculpture emerged from such media as hammered, twisted, or welded steel and bronze.

LITERATURE

In spite of television, book sales increased in the 1950s. This was partly due to the advent of inexpensive paperbacks. When supermarkets and drugstores began selling paperbacks for only a fraction of the cost of hardback volumes, the book-buying public increased.

Military themes were featured in some of the best books of the Fifties. James Jones's *From Here to Eternity* (1951) told about army life in Hawaii. In *The Caine Mutiny* (1954) Herman Wouk depicted the rebellion of an unhappy naval crew against their brutal Captain Queeg.

Earnest Hemingway produced one of his most poignant tales, *The Old Man and the Sea* (1960), a short, moving story of a fisherman. This small book won Hemingway both a Pulitzer Prize and the Nobel Prize for literature.

An engrossing account of the Communist revolution in Russia was *Doctor Zhivago* (1958) by Boris Pasternak. Another best seller with a foreign background was Leon Uris's *Exodus* (1958), the powerful story of the birth of Israel.

One of the most talked about books was Grace Metalious's *Peyton Place* (1956), which dealt with the seamier side of life in a small New England town. Another instant success was J. D. Salinger's novel of rebellious youth, *The Catcher in the Rye* (1951).

Popular nonfiction books of the decade included Carl Sandburg's *Abraham Lincoln* (1954), Anne Morrow Lindbergh's *Gift from the Sea* (1955), and *The Power of Positive Thinking* (1952) by Norman Vincent Peale.

Ernest Hemingway, novelist, short story writer, and journalist, won the Nobel Prize for The Old Man and the Sea *in 1954.*

FASHIONS

During the years immediately following the Second World War, the style of women's clothing was still square shoulders, narrow, short skirts, and flat-hipped straight jackets. But by 1950 women no longer wore clothes that reflected the wartime severity and scarcity of material. The new style had rounded shoulders, tight waists, slightly padded hips, and skirts that reached mid-calf or below. Often the skirts were full and billowy, and some were accompanied by wide, flounced petticoats. Teenagers and older women wore narrow, high-heeled shoes. They teetered about on four-inch heels that narrowed almost to a point.

Short hair was very popular with girls in the Fifties. Many women had wavy permanents, while others had shaggy poodle cuts.

Opposite: notice the clothing of the woman standing in front of the Chevrolet Corvette. She is wearing the typical mid-calf dress of the Fifties. Her tall, high-heeled shoes narrow to a point. Left and below: these scenes from the Seventies hit musical Grease show the clothing and hairstyles of the Fifties.

1955

Above: these singing men of college age seem to reflect the generally happy mood of the Fifties. Notice that all of them have short hair, most of which are "crew cuts." *Right:* this little girl is so intent on twirling her hula hoop that she has not noticed the loss of her underwear.

In the mid-Fifties a revolutionary design swept the fashion world. This was the chemise, or sack dress. Hanging straight and shapeless, the dress denied all feminine curves and gave the appearance of a sack.

As for men's fashions, in 1955 pink suddenly became the rage in shirts. Soon pink appeared in men's ties, hatbands, robes, and even shorts! At school dances throughout the country boys wore charcoal gray suits with full, pleated trousers, pink shirts, and ties with either pink stripes or checks.

During most of the Fifties young men wore their hair military style in short "crew cuts" or "flattops." Toward the end of the decade many boys began copying the Elvis Presley look, including "ducktail" haircuts, black leather jackets, and tight-fitting slacks.

FADS

There were fads galore in the Fifties. Youngsters wore Davy Crockett hats and whirled hula hoops. College boys held zany contests, such as goldfish swallowing and crowding into sports cars and telephone booths. At St. Mary's College in California twenty-two boys claimed a record by cramming into a telephone booth. In Modesto, California, the telephone company provided a special booth into which thirty-two students were jammed. But some claimed that this was not a fair record, since the booth was lying flat on the ground and the telephone had been removed.

People of all ages were saying they spotted flying saucers in the sky. They were also playing Scrabble, and buying many kinds of Chlorophyll green products—toothpaste, stick deodorant, chewing gum, breath fresheners, and cough drops.

Slang expressions that became popular with teenagers were *cool*, meaning "good," and *crazy*, meaning "great." On the other hand, a *square* or a *yo-yo* was a term used for a dull, unattractive person. One widely used expression was *dig*. It could mean to understand ("She digs biology") or to appreciate ("He digs that crazy redhead more than that cool blonde.")

(83)

BASEBALL

On August 12, 1951, as the baseball season was nearing its end, the New York Giants trailed the league-leading Brooklyn Dodgers by thirteen and a half games. Suddenly the Giants caught fire, winning thirty-six of their last forty-seven games, including the final seven in a row. On the last day of the season, the Giants had drawn even with the Dodgers, necessitating a three-game playoff for the National League championship.

The Giants won the first playoff game; the Dodgers the second. In the third game the Dodgers led 4–1 as the teams went into the bottom of the ninth inning. The Giants came to bat for the final time, scored one run, and had men on second and third base with one out.

As Bobby Thomson, the tall, lanky third baseman, came to the plate, the Giants were still trailing 4–2, and the Dodgers were only two outs away from winning the pennant. Thomson took the first fastball for a strike, and then he swung and connected with the

(84)

next fastball. Fans held their breath as his rising line drive shot deep into left field and landed in the stands. Thomson's home run won the game and the pennant for the Giants, and provided a storybook finish to the most astounding comeback in the history of Major League baseball.

The New York Giants and Brooklyn Dodgers made history in another way later in the decade. Both teams deserted New York and moved to the West. As New Yorkers moaned, the Giants took up residence in San Francisco, and Los Angeles became the new home of the Dodgers. While the Dodgers waited for their new stadium to be built, they drew record crowds to the Los Angeles Coliseum, a huge stadium used mainly for football games and track meets.

Bobby Thomson, hitting the home run that brought the Giants the 1951 pennant and climaxed the greatest come-back perform-ance of a base-ball team in major league history.

Above left: Joe DiMaggio, born in California in 1914. Nicknamed the "Yankee Clipper" by his fans, Joe was elected to the Baseball Hall of Fame in 1955. Above right: Mickey Mantle was born in Oklahoma in 1931. He was named Most Valuable Player in the American League in 1956, 1957, and 1962. Above middle: Willie Mays was voted the National League's Most Valuable Player in 1954 and again in 1965. For several years he led the league in home runs and stolen bases. Right: Roy Campanella was one of the superstars, both as a hitter and catcher. In 1958 Roy was paralyzed from an automobile accident. Here he is shown at a fan appreciation night with managers Walter Alston (left) of the Dodgers and Casey Stengel (right) of the Yankees.

But the greatest baseball team of the Fifties was the New York Yankees, with the old professor Casey Stengel as manager. During Stengel's twelve years at the helm (1948–60), his Yankees won ten pennants and seven world championships, including five world series in a row. In the 1956 world series a Yankee hurler, Don Larsen, pitched a no-hit, no-run game. It was the only perfect game in world series history.

Stengel managed some of the brightest stars in baseball, such as Joe DiMaggio, Mickey Mantle, Yogi Berra, and Whitey Ford. Other players in the decade who were among baseball's superstars included the Giants' Willie Mays, Stan Musial of the St. Louis Cardinals, Ted Williams of the Boston Red Sox, and the Dodgers' Jackie Robinson and Roy Campanella.

FOOTBALL

Sports authorities claim that the greatest professional football game ever played occurred when the Baltimore Colts faced the New York Giants for the championship on December 28, 1958. At halftime the Colts led 14–3, but the Giants charged back with two touchdowns to move ahead, 17–14. With only seven seconds left, Baltimore kicked a field goal to tie the score and send the game into a "sudden death" overtime period. Then Colt quarterback Johnny Unitas mixed short passes and runs, driving his team from its own twenty-yard line to the winning touchdown. It has often been said that this single exciting televised game turned millions of American fans onto professional football and caused it to become the number one sports attraction on television.

The dominant team in professional American football for most of the decade was the Cleveland Browns. In the early Fifties the Browns were led by a superb passing quarterback, Otto Graham. During the ten years that Graham played he engineered the Browns to ten consecutive division titles and seven championships.

In 1957 the Browns acquired a magnificent fullback, Jim Brown, who is rated by many experts as the best ball-carrier football has ever known. Brown averaged more than five yards every time he carried the ball. He set an amazing record by gaining 12,312 yards during his nine-year career at Cleveland.

In college football Oklahoma was the outstanding team of the decade, winning forty-seven games in a row between 1953 and 1957. This incredible winning streak was finally broken by Notre Dame, 7–0, in November 1957.

TRACK AND FIELD

An "impossible" track barrier was broken at Oxford, England, on May 6, 1954. A twenty-five-year-old medical student, Roger Bannister, started the mile run. Three minutes, 59.4 seconds later he crossed the finish line to become the first man in history to break the four-minute mile. His feat was acclaimed as the "sports story of the century."

About six weeks later another runner, John Landy of Australia, broke Bannister's new record by running the mile in a blazing time of 3:58. Later in the same year Bannister and Landy met in the British Empire games. Landy set the early pace, but Bannister's finishing kick swept him to victory. In the race both men again broke the four-minute mile.

Two days after Bannister first set the mile record, American Parry O'Brien broke another track barrier. He became the first man in history to put the shot more than sixty feet. Moreover, he did it three times in one afternoon, and on his final toss the iron ball went a distance of sixty feet, five and a quarter inches. O'Brien used a new technique in achieving his world mark. Instead of launching his effort from the traditional position of standing at a right angle to the direction in which he would throw, O'Brien began with his back to the toeboard, thus putting all his force into a 180-degree turn rather than one of a mere 90 degrees.

Left: Jim Brown of the
Cleveland Browns was
the greatest football
runner in the Fifties.
Above: sports history
was made in 1954
when Roger Bannister
became the first man
in history to run the
mile in less than four
minutes.

In 1956 still another long-standing record fell. Charles Dumas, a nineteen-year-old high jumper from Compton, California, soared over the bar at seven feet and one-half inches to set a new world mark.

Another Californian achieved fame in a grueling event in the Olympic Games. In 1948 Bob Mathias won the Olympic decathlon, and in 1952 he took another gold medal in the same event. Mathias became the only man ever to win the Olympic decathlon twice.

BASKETBALL

Basketball laurels in the 1950s were divided between two professional teams, the Minneapolis Lakers and the Boston Celtics. Led by six-foot, ten-inch George Mikan, the Lakers won three straight titles early in the decade. Mikan was named by a popular magazine as the greatest basketball player in the first half of the twentieth century.

Mikan retired after the 1953–54 season, and soon a new professional basketball dynasty began at Boston. Bob Cousy, Bill Sharman, and Tom Heinsohn were among the stars of the Celtic team. But their fabulous superstar was Bill Russell, a black player who in college had led the University of San Francisco to an unprecedented fifty-five straight victories and two national championships. Beginning with the 1958–59 season, the Boston Celtics won the National Basketball Association Championship eight years in a row.

TENNIS

Pancho Gonzales was probably the best male tennis player in the Fifties, but most of the headlines were captured by the women tennis stars. At age sixteen Maureen Connolly won the National Women's Singles Championship in 1951, thus becoming the youngest national tennis champion since 1901. Two years later "Little

Mo" won the Grand Slam of tennis—the Australian, French, Wimbledon, and U.S. titles.

Althea Gibson was the first black invited to compete in the U.S. Lawn Tennis Association's National Championship. That was in 1950, and she was eliminated in the second round. But Althea kept trying, although she was handicapped in finding top-flight competition because only a few tournaments were open to blacks. Finally, in 1957 at the age of thirty, she won both the U.S. and Wimbledon crowns. Althea Gibson, who erased the racial barrier in tennis, repeated her double victory the following year.

The two top women tennis players in the Fifties were Althea Gibson (left) and Maureen Connolly (right). In this picture Miss Connolly has just missed the ball, but she went on to win the match and the national single's title in 1953.

GOLF

Two of the most heroic athletes in the 1950s were golfers. In 1949 Ben Hogan was badly injured in a near fatal automobile accident. Doctors doubted that he would ever walk normally again, let alone play golf. But they did not reckon with Hogan's gutty determination. Limping with pain, he courageously returned to the links.

In 1950, only seventeen months after his accident, Hogan won the U.S. Open. The following year he took both the U.S. Open and the Masters, and in 1953 he won three of golf's four biggest tournaments.

Babe Didrikson won more acclaim in more sports than any other athlete in history, male or female. She won Olympic gold medals in track, All-America basketball and softball awards, and thirty-three golf tournaments, including three U.S. Women's Opens. The Associated Press in 1950 proclaimed Babe Didrikson the most outstanding woman athlete of the first half-century.

In 1953 Babe was stricken with cancer, and her doctors said she could never play golf again. But she defied this grim conclusion. In 1954 she fired an incredible 291 to win the U.S. Women's Open by twelve strokes. Then she went on to pick up six more tournament victories before her death in 1956.

The stories of how Ben Hogan and Babe Didrikson overcame almost insurmountable odds will live forever in the annals of great sports history.

*Courageous Babe Didrikson
is shown here in the
1954 Women's National
Open Golf Championship.*

(93)

Index

About the Author

Edmund Lindop is a high school social studies teacher, author of many books and articles, and a respected historian. For Franklin Watts he has previously authored *The Dazzling Twenties*, *The Turbulent Thirties*, and *The First Book of Elections*. Mr. Lindop lives with his wife, Esther, who is also an author and a teacher, and his daughter Laurie, in Pacific Palisades, California.